Science

Vocabulary Readers

Tornadoes!

D0115503

Justin McCory Martin

SCHOLASTIC INC.

NEW YORK • TORONTO • LONDON • AUCKLAND • SYDNEY
MEXICO CITY • NEW DELHI • HONG KONG • BUENOS AIRES

ISBN: 0-439-87641-9

Photos Credits
Cover: © Don Farrall/Photodisc/Getty Images; title page: © Eric Nguyen/Jim Reed Photography/Photo Researchers; contents page, top: © Aaron Horowitz/Corbis; contents page, middle: © Jim Reed/Getty Images; contents page, bottom: © Jim Reed/Corbis; page 4: © Aaron Horowitz/Corbis; page 5: © Warren Faidley/Weatherstock; page 6: © Eric Meola/Getty Images; page 7: © A. T. Willett/Getty Images; page 8: © Jim Reed/Getty Images; page 9: © Phillip Simpson/Getty Images; page 10: © Stephen Frink/Getty Images; page 11: © Weatherstock/Peter Arnold; page 11, inset: © Patrick Richardson/Great Bend Tribune/AP/Wide World Photos; page 12: © Brendan Smialowski/Getty Images; page 13: © Jim Reed/Corbis; page 14: © Eric Nguyen/Jim Reed Photography/Photo Researchers; page 15: © Lester Lefkowitz/Getty Images; back cover: © Eric Nguyen/Jim Reed Photography/Corbis.

Photo research by Nancy Choi
Design by Holly Grundon

12 11 10 9 8 7 6 5 4 3 2 1   6 7 8 9 10 11/0

Printed in China
First printing, October 2006

Contents

Chapter 1
What Is a Tornado?

Page 4

Chapter 2
Tornado Types

Page 8

Chapter 3
Storm Warnings

Page 12

Glossary and Comprehension Questions
Page 16

What Is a Tornado?

What twists and twirls and tears through the air? A **tornado**! Let's learn all about them.

The shape of a tornado is called a funnel.

A thunderstorm can make the wind spin around and around. Sometimes those whirling winds turn into a tornado. A tornado is huge! It looks like an elephant's trunk.

Fast Fact

Tornadoes are also called twisters and whirlwinds.

Tornadoes spin superfast. Look out! Anything a tornado touches can be blown apart by the strong winds.

This picture shows a tornado twisting through Texas.

Tornadoes can be very loud. Some sound like freight trains. Rumble, rumble!

Chapter 2

Tornado Types

This picture shows a tornado in the country.

Tornadoes can happen anywhere. Some whirl through the country. Some whoosh through towns and cities.

This picture shows a dust devil.

Some tornadoes happen in the desert. These dirty tornadoes are called dust devils.

This picture shows a waterspout.

Tornadoes can even happen over water. They are called waterspouts. A waterspout can pick up a fish and drop it many miles away!

wedge tornado

rope tornado

Tornadoes come in different shapes and sizes. Fat ones are called wedge tornadoes. Skinny ones are called rope tornadoes.

Chapter 3

Storm Warnings

This home was hit by a tornado.

Tornadoes are very dangerous. They can knock down trees and power lines. They can smash houses!

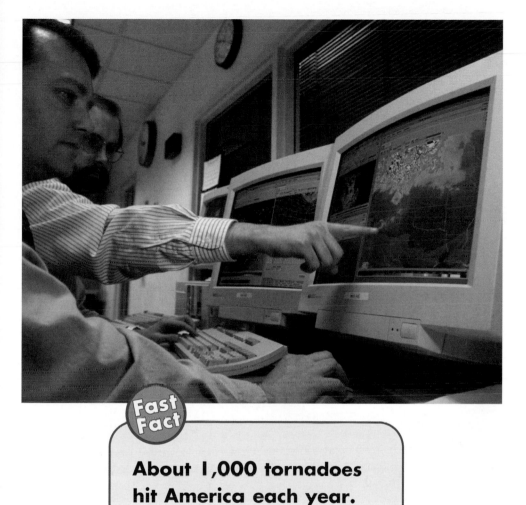

Fast Fact

About 1,000 tornadoes
hit America each year.

Special scientists look out for tornadoes.
When they think one is coming, they warn
everyone.

Where should you stay during a tornado? **Storm cellars**, basements, and rooms without windows are the safest spots.

Fast Fact

Some tornadoes last only a few seconds!

Rumble, rumble! Tornadoes are powerful storms! The good news is that most of them last less than ten minutes. Then the loud, whirling winds are all gone.

Glossary

dust devil (**duhst dev**-uhl): a small tornado of whirling dust

funnel (**fuhn**-uhl): a shape that is wide at the top and narrow at the bottom

rope tornado (**rohp** tor-**nay**-doh): a thin tornado that looks like a rope

storm cellar (**storm sel**-ur): a room belowground

tornado (tor-**nay**-doh): a wild, whirling column of air

waterspout (**wah**-tur-**spout**): a tornado that happens over warm water

wedge tornado (**wej** tor-**nay**-doh): a fat tornado

Comprehension Questions

1. Can you describe a tornado's shape?

2. Can you name two kinds of tornadoes?

3. Can you share three more facts about tornadoes?